Written by Rachel Elliot
Illustrated by Madison Mastrangelo

First published 2017 by Parragon Books, Ltd.
Copyright © 2019 Cottage Door Press, LLC
5005 Newport Drive, Rolling Meadows, Illinois 60008

ISBN 978-1-68052-552-6

Parragon Books is an imprint of Cottage Door Press, LLC.
Parragon Books® and the Parragon® logo are
registered trademarks of Cottage Door Press, LLC.

IN THE BEGINNING

The Story of Creation

PaRragon.

In the beginning, before time began, there was nothing. Nothing to see. Nothing to hear. Nothing to touch or smell. There was only silence. God moved alone through the inky darkness.

Then God created the heavens and the Earth, and the Earth was covered by water.

"Let there be light," God said.

It was faint at first, a flicker in the darkness that grew and grew. It became a glowing ball that pushed the gloom aside, soft and yellow, then red, pink, and dazzling gold.

God delighted in its loveliness. The changing light seemed to have a life of its own, and God called it "day." When the light faded into darkness, He named it "night."

It was the very first day of the world.

On the second day, when the light came back, God made the sky. It was a soft, bright blue, and it hung over the Earth like a canopy.

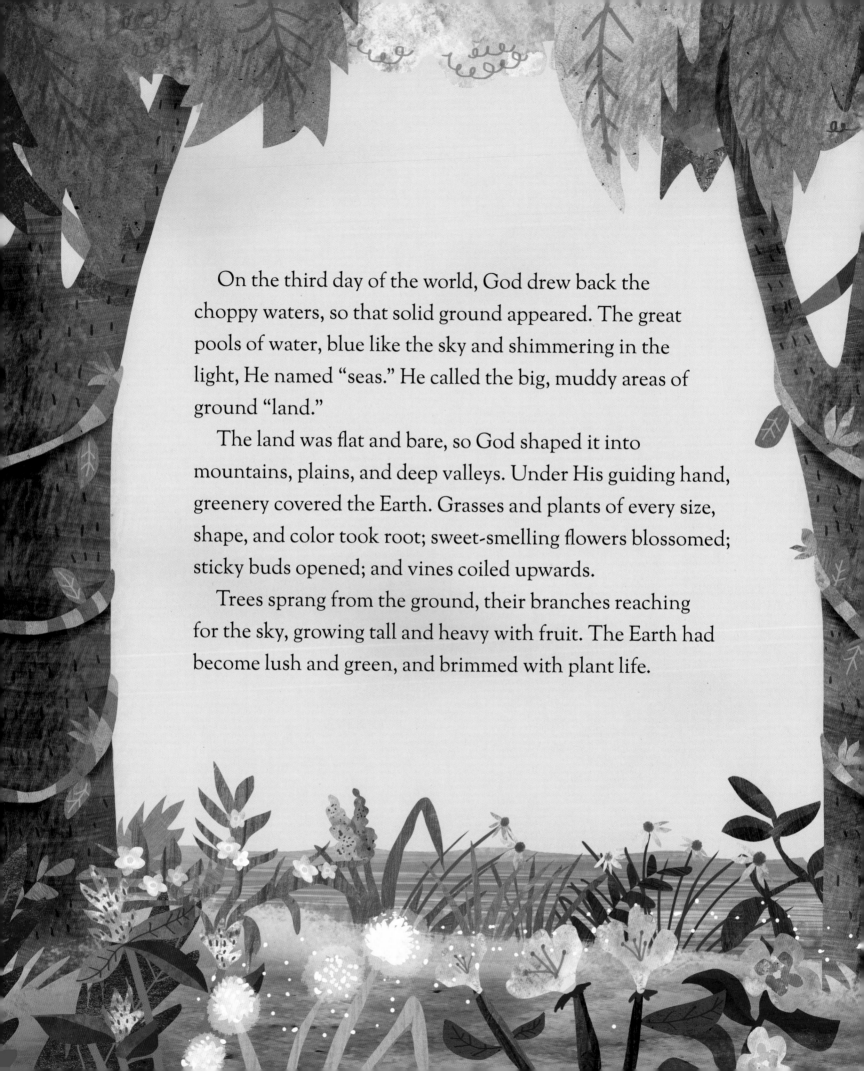

On the third day of the world, God drew back the choppy waters, so that solid ground appeared. The great pools of water, blue like the sky and shimmering in the light, He named "seas." He called the big, muddy areas of ground "land."

The land was flat and bare, so God shaped it into mountains, plains, and deep valleys. Under His guiding hand, greenery covered the Earth. Grasses and plants of every size, shape, and color took root; sweet-smelling flowers blossomed; sticky buds opened; and vines coiled upwards.

Trees sprang from the ground, their branches reaching for the sky, growing tall and heavy with fruit. The Earth had become lush and green, and brimmed with plant life.

On the fourth day, God said, "Let there be signs to mark the day and night."

He made the fiery Sun to show the day and the gentle Moon to shine at night. During the day, the Moon hid in the shadows. At night, the Sun turned its golden face away, while the Moon cast its silvery beams over the land.

God also brightened the night sky with millions upon millions of tiny glittering stars. He felt pleased with the beautiful world He had created.

God's new world was a peaceful land filled with flowers, trees, and rushing rivers, but there were no birds to perch in the trees. There were no bees to buzz from flower to flower, nor fish to leap through the waves. The only sounds were the whisper of the wind among the leaves and the waves

On the fifth day, God filled the waters with living creatures. Suddenly, the sea teemed with fish that moved as one. He made whales that sent great plumes of spray high up into the sky, and dolphins that leaped playfully in and out of the waves.

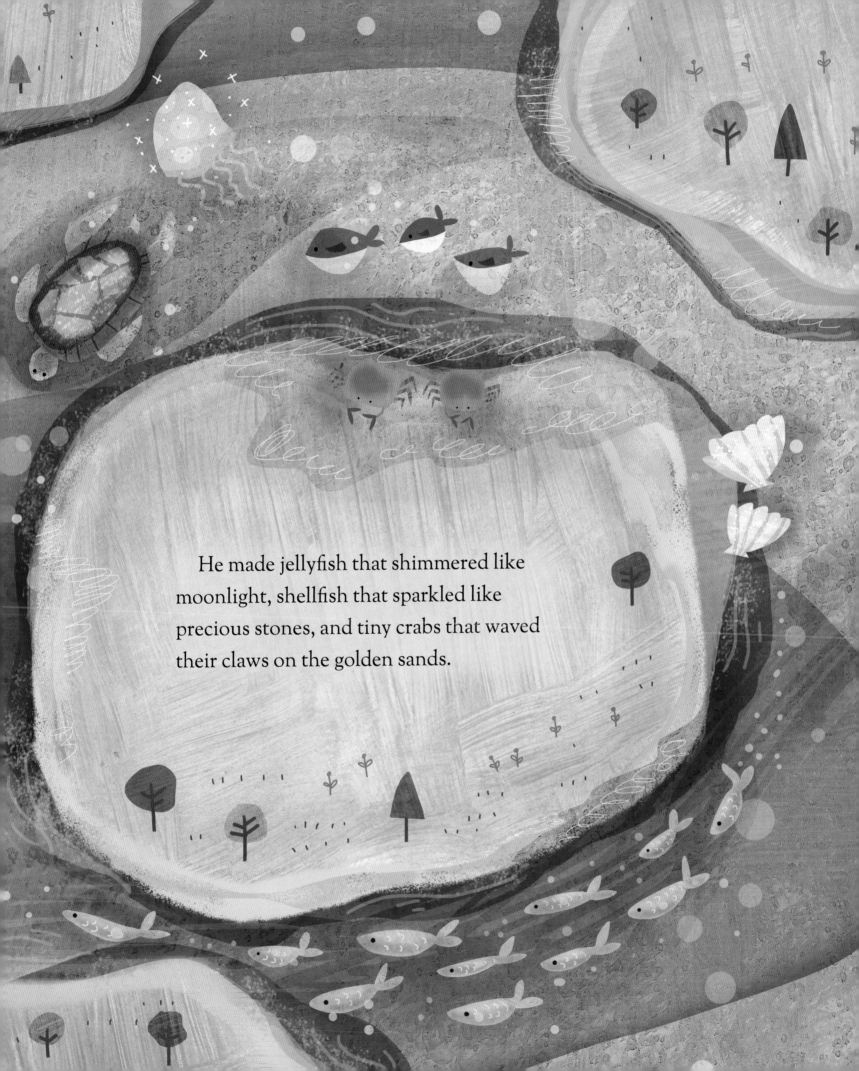

He made jellyfish that shimmered like moonlight, shellfish that sparkled like precious stones, and tiny crabs that waved their claws on the golden sands.

Then God said, "Let there be creatures of the air that will fill the sky with life."

There began a great fluttering of feathers and flapping of wings, and a cloud of birds and insects of all shapes and sizes rose into the sky. Tiny chirruping sparrows mingled with colorful parakeets and silent, gliding hawks. The sky was alive with color and sound as the twittering birds found shelter among the trees and bushes, discovered fruit, and washed their feathers in the bright streams. Their happy songs filled God's ears, and He blessed them.

On the sixth day of the world, God said, "Now, let there be creatures on the land!" and the Earth began to shake with the thunder of a thousand feet.

The world hummed with voices large and small, jostling to be heard. Regal lions prowled beside mighty elephants and rhinos. Monkeys swung through the trees, cackling to each other, and bears lumbered through the undergrowth.

Fierce animals paced side by side with the gentlest of God's creatures. Everyone, from the tiny shrews to the tall giraffes, was looking for a new home. Some liked the cool of the snowy mountains, and some preferred the heat of the rain forests. Snakes slithered into the jungles, crocodiles hid in rivers, and squirrels climbed tall trees. The world pulsed with life.

God looked around and was happy with what He saw.
But something was missing.

"Who will care for all the animals?" God asked Himself.

He took handfuls of earth and shaped a creature who looked like Him. He breathed life into him and called him "man." Then he took a rib from the man. With the rib, God created "woman." The man and woman opened their eyes and stared around them in wonder. Slowly, they stretched their arms and legs, and rose to their feet. They stood in front of God, holding hands, as beautiful and innocent as the new world.

God blessed them, and named the man Adam and the woman Eve.

"Your job is to look after the wonders I have created," He said. "You will rule over the fish in the sea, the birds in the sky, and every creature on the Earth. You will have fruit to eat and water to drink. I want you to enjoy your life here."

God's work was done. The world was every bit as beautiful as He had imagined.

It was the seventh day, and God rested.

Next, God made a beautiful garden for Adam and Eve, and named it Eden. There were flowers, and trees full of delicious fruit to eat, and velvet-soft grass to lie on. A sparkling stream gave Adam and Eve clean water to drink.

There was a huge tree in the middle of the garden. Its branches reached into the sky like upstretched arms, and God named it the Tree of Knowledge.

"You can pick fruit from any tree in the garden, except the Tree of Knowledge," He told Adam and Eve. "If you eat from that tree, you will die."

Adam and Eve listened to everything God told them. They had all that they needed and they were happy. They cared for the animals and the garden, just as God had told them.

One day, Eve was picking berries near the Tree of Knowledge when she heard rustling in the leaves of the tree. A snake was watching her, its tongue flicking in and out.

"Sssmell the sssweet fruit," the snake hissed. "Try it. Tassste it!"

"No," Eve replied. "God has told us we must not eat the fruit from the Tree of Knowledge or we will die."

The snake shook its head. "It would make you as wissse as God," it said. "Jussst one bite would make you a goddessss."

The snake's words made
Eve long to try it. Slowly,
she plucked a ripe fruit and
drew it toward her. It smelled
sweet and delicious. Her
heart thumped with fear and
excitement.

Eve could not resist. She took a tiny bite of the fruit. Adam saw her and, although he knew that it was wrong, he burned with curiosity. So Eve handed him the fruit and he tried it. Smiling, the snake slithered away.

God knew at once what Adam and Eve had done. He was upset and angry.

"You must leave Eden," He told them. "From now on, the lives of humankind will be full of trouble and worry. Now that you have eaten from the Tree of Knowledge, your bodies will eventually die. But I will find a way to save you."

Adam and Eve shivered and wept as they left Eden behind them. Greed had taken them from a place of gentle breezes to a cruel world where the wind bit and the rain soaked their bodies.

But God, who loves His people, gave Adam and Eve something very special. He gave them hope. Perhaps one day, He told them, humankind might yet return to the beautiful garden of Eden and to the love of God.